FEEDING THE WORLD
Rice

Feeding the World

CORN

DAIRY PRODUCTS

EGGS

FARMED FISH

MEAT

RICE

SOYBEANS

WHEAT

FEEDING THE WORLD

Rice

JANE E. SINGER

MASON CREST

Mason Crest
450 Parkway Drive, Suite D
Broomall, PA 19008
www.masoncrest.com

Printed and bound in the United States of America.

First printing
9 8 7 6 5 4 3 2 1

Series ISBN: 978-1-4222-2741-1
ISBN: 978-1-4222-2747-3
ebook ISBN: 978-1-4222-9079-8

The Library of Congress has cataloged the

hardcopy format(s) as follows:

Library of Congress Cataloging-in-Publication Data

Singer, Jane E.
    Rice / Jane E. Singer.
        p. cm. — (Feeding the world)
    ISBN 978-1-4222-2747-3 (hardcover) — ISBN 978-1-4222-2741-1 (series) — ISBN 978-1-4222-9079-8 (ebook)
    1. Rice—Juvenile literature. 2. Food supply—Juvenile literature. I. Title. II. Series: Feeding the world.
    SB191.R5S5878 2014
    633.1'8—dc23
                                    2013004741

Publisher's notes:
The websites mentioned in this book were active at the time of publication. The publisher is not responsible for websites that have changed their addresses or discontinued operation since the date of publication. The publisher will review and update the website addresses each time the book is reprinted.

CONTENTS

CHAPTER ONE

Where Does Rice Come From?

What do you know about your food? You know that it tastes good (or not). You know that you need to eat it to live. You know you can eat food at home or in a restaurant.

But do you know where food comes from? Yes, it comes from a grocery store. But before that, it comes from somewhere else. Your food has a long story.

AT THE STORE

Imagine you're walking through a grocery store. Think about all the different kinds of food you walk by.

Maybe you head past the fresh fruits and vegetables first. All of those fruits and vegetables grew in the ground. They all came from the earth.

Those fruits and vegetables grew on farms. Farmers are in charge of growing them. Farmers plant seeds. They take care of the plants that grow. After some time, they **harvest** the fruits and vegetables that grow from those plants.

Next, you walk by the meat. Meat comes from animals. Beef used to be cow. Pork used to be pig.

Cows and pigs and other meat animals are raised on farms. Animal farmers take care of them and raise them. The pigs and cows and other animals also eat food that came from farms. They eat grass and corn and other plants that grow in the ground.

Now you walk over to the dairy section. Dairy **products** are foods made from animal milk. There are lots of milk, yogurt, sour cream, butter, and more. A farmer raised some cows, goats, or other animals. Then she milked them. The milk ended up in a factory that made it into cheese or butter or another dairy product.

Finally, you walk over to the chips and cookies and frozen foods. All that stuff is called processed food. Processed foods are foods that are made in factories. Someone has to put a bunch of **ingredients** together to make a processed food. Processed foods don't grow in the ground. You can't go to a farm and pick a bottle of juice from a tree. You can't dig up a can of soup from the ground. But the ingredients in processed foods do come from the earth. Let's think about a cookie.

There are lots of ingredients in a cookie. Cookies have flour in them. Flour is made from crushed-up wheat, which is a kind of grain. Cookies have sugar. They might also have baking powder, eggs, and chocolate chips.

GROW YOUR OWN

If you are really curious about where food comes from, grow some yourself! It's pretty easy to grow a garden full of veggies. If you don't have a yard, you can plant vegetables in pots too. Just get a bunch of seeds and plant them in dirt. Your seeds will need sunlight and water to grow. See what happens. Choose vegetables you know you already like. Or choose some you haven't tried before. Watch as your seeds grow into tomatoes, beans, lettuce, and more. You'll be able to see for yourself how your food grows!

8   **Rice**

All the food you see in the supermarket has a story. Many people had to work very hard to get food to the supermarket where you and your family shop. You can't pick a bag of potato chips from a tree, but the things that go into potato chips are grown on farms.

Farmers help to raise the animals that give us milk and meat. Without farmers raising cows for milk, we wouldn't have foods like ice cream, yogurt, butter, or cheese. Farmers are an important part of your food's story.

Farmers grow the wheat for flour. Other farmers grow sugarcane that becomes sugar. Still other farmers raise the chickens that lay the eggs and the cows that give the milk. More farmers raise cacao beans, which become chocolate. Workers in factories make the baking powder.

All those ingredients end up in factories. Workers in the factories make the cookies. Then it ends up in the grocery store. After a while, you buy a package and bring the cookies home.

10   Rice

PEOPLE MAKE YOUR FOOD

Plants and animals and dirt are all part of the story of your food. People are a big part of that story too. Lots of people help your food get from a farm to your plate.

First, there are the farmers. Farmers take care of growing things. Some grow vegetables. Some grow fruit. Others raise animals for meat or eggs or milk.

Farmers could have really big farms or really tiny farms. Some farmers only grow enough food for their families. Other farmers have huge farms that grow food for grocery stores.

After the farmer is done growing his crops or his animals, other people take over. A truck driver comes to the farm to pick up the food.

The truck driver takes the food to a factory. There are lots of workers in a factory. Some workers take the food off the truck. Some take care of machines that mix up the ingredients and make them into a new food. Others check the food to make sure it is healthy and won't make people sick.

After that, another truck driver comes to pick up the new food from the factory. She might take it to a plane or a boat or a train. That's what happens if the food is going to be sent far away.

She might bring it to a grocery store warehouse. Grocery stores own big warehouses. They bring lots of food there. The food is sorted. Then it's sent out to all the grocery stores in one area.

At the grocery store, workers take the food off the truck. They put it on the shelves. Then you come to buy it!

RICE

All over the world, people eat rice every day. Rice is a grain. Grains are the seeds of certain plants. Oats, wheat, and barley are other kinds of grains.

Each piece of rice is one seed. If you planted a rice seed, it would grow into a rice plant. Rice plants look kind of like giant grass. In fact, all grains are related to grass plants.

Like other grains, rice is grown on farms. Farmers and farmworkers work hard to get you the rice you eat. Most rice is grown in fields covered in water. These fields are called rice paddies. Most rice needs a lot of water to grow well. A few kinds of rice grow on dry land. Rice also needs hot weather. It can't really grow in cold places.

Rice is often grown in fields covered in water. Just as people eat rice all over the world, farmers grow rice in many different countries. This rice farm is in Thailand, for example.

12   Rice

After the farm, rice gets processed. The outside has to be taken off. We can't eat the outside. Sometimes rice goes through more steps in a factory too.

After it's processed, rice travels to where it will be made into other foods or sold to hungry people. The rice might travel just a few hours away from where it was grown. Or it could travel all the way around the world!

Each type of food has a story. These stories explain how the food got to your plate. Rice is no different. Rice takes a long trip before it gets to your plate!

CHAPTER TWO

The History of Rice

Rice has been around for a long time. And it has become one of the most important foods in the world. People from almost every part of the world eat rice. How did rice become so important?

RICE IN THE PAST

We know that people were eating rice at least 4,000 years ago. But people might have been eating it even earlier than that. No one knows for sure. No one wrote things down back then. We just have to guess.

The first rice was eaten in India and China. In fact, in the old Chinese language, the word for growing rice and the word for farming is the same. When people thought of farming, they thought of rice.

Today, we believe that people in India were the first to find wild rice plants. They tried tasting them and the rice was good! Rice had a lot of the things that people needed to eat to stay healthy, so eating rice helped people survive.

People have been growing rice in China for thousands of years. Many things about farming have changed over time, but people still farm rice in flooded fields. Here, farmers plant rice seeds by hand, just as people have for a very long time.

 **16** **Rice**

Next, people had to figure out how to grow rice themselves. Before farming, they had to find it in the wild. Then they had to pick it. Then they had to carry it all the way back to where they lived. It would be a lot easier if they could grow it on farms. They would always know where it was. And they wouldn't have to travel very far to get it.

We think that farmers first started growing rice in China. Chinese farmers were the first to farm rice paddies. Rice paddies are a way of growing rice in a field flooded with water. Rice grows in land covered by water.

RICE MYTHS

Many people have stories about rice. The stories explain where rice came from and why people eat it. One story from China tells us that a huge flood killed all the plants that people ate. Everyone was hungry because there wasn't any food. One day, a dog came to the people. It had rice hanging from its tail. The people decided to plant the rice to see what would happen. The rice grew and grew. Soon, people could eat it. After that, people weren't hungry anymore.

TRAVELING RICE

Asia didn't keep rice a secret forever. After some time, rice spread west. It was such a good food that new people got excited about eating it all the time.

Growing and eating rice spread out from China and India to the rest of Asia first. Then people started growing rice in the Mediterranean. People grew it in Greece and Spain. They grew it in North Africa. Rice didn't grow in northern Europe though, because the weather there was too cold.

Pretty soon, rice ended up across the ocean. In the 1500s, lots of Europeans started going to the Americas. They brought the food people ate in Europe with them. One of those foods was rice. People started growing rice in Central and South America.

A little later on, people started growing rice in North America too. Rice can't grow well in the colder parts of North America, so it was mostly grown in the south of the United States.

Today, many rice farmers use machines to help them work faster. Machines like these help farmers harvest much more rice much faster than they could by themselves.

 **18** **Rice**

RICE TODAY

Today, rice is grown on every continent of the world except Antarctica. Rice spread a lot from just one part of Asia. Most people on Earth have probably eaten rice at some point in their lives.

The way we grow rice has changed over time. For most of the time people have been eating rice, we picked it by hand. It was hard to get the outside shell off. It took a lot of time to harvest rice.

Now, some rice farmers use machines. The machines harvest the rice all at once. They can take the hard outsides off. It makes harvesting rice a lot faster. We can grow more of it these days.

Scientists are also always working on growing new kinds of rice. They can create rice that grows better in the cold. Or rice that needs less water. Or rice that is bigger. They hope that new rice will make rice farming easier and will make rice farmers more money.

Today, there are big rice farms and small rice farms. There are even new kinds of rice. But the biggest change of all is that so many people all over the world eat rice now!

The History of Rice   19

CHAPTER THREE

Who Grows the Rice We Eat?

There isn't just one kind of rice farmer. Rice farmers live all over the world. They have different kinds of farms. They have different ways of growing rice. But they all grow the same thing!

BY COUNTRY

Rice was first eaten in Asia. And that's where it's grown and eaten the most today. Out of all the rice in the world, 90 percent comes from Asia. That means if you had ten bags of rice, nine of them would be from somewhere in Asia.

China and India grow half the world's rice. Farmers in both of these countries grow rice for the people that live there. They also grow rice for people in other countries. Lots of rice is sent to places that don't grow so much rice.

Other Asian countries grow a lot of rice too. Lots of rice comes from Indonesia, Bangladesh, Vietnam, Thailand, and more.

Another area that grows rice is in Latin America. Brazil grows the most rice in Latin America.

EATING RICE

Asia doesn't just grow the most rice. People from Asia eat the most rice, too! Depending on what country they're from, people in Asia eat between 200 and 400 pounds (90 and 180 kilograms) of rice every year!

In countries around the world, rice is cooked in different ways and used in different kinds of food. Rice is very important in food in many Asian countries.

22   **Rice**

Many farmers plant their rice by hand. Even small farms have many rice plants, so there's a lot of work for farmers!

BIG FARMS, LITTLE FARMS

Farmers grow rice on all sorts of farms all over the world. In Asia, a lot of the farms are very small. Farmers might work by themselves, or with a few other people to grow rice on a small farm.

Farmers have a lot to do on small farms. They flood their fields (because most rice grows in ground covered by water). They plant their seeds by hand. They take care of the **seedlings**.

When the rice is ready to harvest, farmers do that by hand too. They cut the rice off of the plant. They get the rice ready to sell. A rice farmer on a small farm gets to be part of every step of growing and harvesting her rice.

On bigger farms, machines help to plant the rice. On this Japanese rice farm, farmers use machines like this one to plant lots of rice at once.

24 **Rice**

Even though they work hard, small rice farmers often do not make much money. They farm because their families have farmed for a long time. It's part of who they are.

Other farmers work on bigger farms. There are lots of people who work on these rice farms. There might even be more than one farmer.

Everything is done with machines on big farms. The farmer has to keep track of lots more rice, and has to make sure all the machines are working. It can be very different from working on a small rice farm.

ORGANIC FARMERS

Have you ever had organic food? Many farmers that grow rice or other foods use chemicals on their farms. They use them to kill bugs and weeds. They use them to keep the soil healthy. But not all farmers want to use chemicals. Chemicals can get into the water and poison animals and other creatures (including humans). Pesticides kill all bugs, even though some bugs are good for the farm, like bees and spiders. Farmers who don't want to use chemicals choose to grow organically. They don't use chemical pesticides and fertilizers that could hurt the environment. Organic farmers work with nature to grow food.

Organic farms are found all over the world. They are often smaller than non-organic farms, but that isn't always true. Organic farming is growing in popularity. There are organic vegetables, fruit, grains, meat, and more. Maybe you've even eaten some organic food from the grocery store or the farmers' market. Organic food has a label that says it's organic. Take a look the next time you're at the store.

CHAPTER FOUR

How Is Rice Grown?

There are lots of different rice farmers. They all grow rice. And they all do the same things. They get the dirt ready, plant the seeds, help the rice grow, and harvest it. But different farmers do things differently.

TYPES OF FARMS

There are four different kinds of rice farms. Farmers choose which kind of farm to have based on where they live.

One kind of rice farm is called **irrigated**. On irrigated farms, the land that the rice grows on is covered by water. The farmer can control how much water is covering up the rice. Usually there's only a little bit of water.

Most rice farms in China and other places in East Asia are irrigated. Most of the rice grown in the world grows on these farms.

GROWING YOUR OWN RICE!

You don't have to be a rice farmer to grow rice. Ask your parents if you can try growing your own and see what happens. First, you need some containers that don't have holes in the bottom. Then get some long-grain brown rice from the store (white rice won't grow). Fill up your container with about six inches of dirt. Add enough water so that it is two inches above the dirt. Then, sprinkle a handful of rice in the container. You want the rice to sink and sit on the dirt. If you live in a warm place, keep the container outside in the sun. If it's not that warm outside, keep it inside in the sun. The goal is to keep your rice as warm as possible. Your rice should grow and grow. When it's a few inches high, add more water so that it is four inches above the dirt. Then let the water go down. Your rice will be ready to harvest when the plants become yellow. There shouldn't be much water left in the container. Cut the plants and lay them out to dry in a warm place for a couple weeks. Finally, put them in the oven at 100 degrees for an hour or so. You'll have to pick off all the outsides shells by hand. Then you're ready to cook and eat your rice!

Another kind of rice farm is called a rain-fed farm. On rain-fed farms, the rice is also covered up by water. But the farmer can't control it. She just has to depend on how much rain comes down.

Rain-fed farms are dry some of the year. Then, when there's lots of rain, it gets flooded. There could be a lot of water on one farm. You can find rain-fed farms in India, Indonesia, the Philippines, and more.

Deepwater rice farms are a little like rain-fed farms. Farmers don't control how much water floods their fields. But on deepwater farms, there's a lot of water. The whole plant gets covered up with water!

There aren't a whole lot of deepwater farms. But there are some in Southeast Asia. It's harder to grow rice on deepwater farms.

The last kind of rice farm is called upland. On upland farms there isn't any water covering the field.

Farmers raising rice on flooded fields have to make sure walls between fields are built well. Farmers use the walls to make sure water doesn't spill into another field.

This Chinese rice farmer plows his fields with help from a buffalo. The buffalo drags the plow behind it. The plow breaks up the soil and makes it better for growing things.

Rice farmers in Latin America and West Africa have upland farms. There isn't as much water around. The fields don't get flooded.

PREPARING THE DIRT

Planting anything starts with the ground. For rice that's going to be grown in water, the ground has to be plowed. Plowing means to stir up the **soil** and put air into it. It helps seeds grow better.

On small farms, farmers plow with a big animal, like a water buffalo. They hook up a plow to the buffalo, and it pulls it along. On bigger farms, big tractors do the plowing instead of animals.

Then the farmer has to make the soil healthier. He might add something called compost, which is plants that have rotted and turned into something that looks like dirt. He might add animal poop.

Compost starts as old bits of food or dead plants. After a while, the compost starts to look like dirt. Adding compost to a field can help the soil stay healthy. Healthy soil makes for better crops!

Some farmers grow rice on terraces. Rice terraces are fields that are on the side of a hill. The fields look kind of like steps up the hill, with rice growing on each one.

The poop fertilizes the dirt. Fertilizers help things grow by keeping the dirt healthy. All these things add **nutrients** into the soil. Seeds need them to grow, just like you do!

If the field is going to be flooded, the farmer has to do some work before that. He has to make sure the field can be flooded. It has to keep all the water in. One choice is to build walls around the field. Every year, he has to make sure the walls are still standing.

PLANTING THE SEEDS

After flooding the field, the farmer plants the seeds. She might plant seeds in a special area just for tiny seedlings. When the seedlings get big, she digs them up and plants them in the big field where she wants them.

At first, rice looks like a kind of grass growing from the flooded fields of a rice farm. These seedlings will grow into taller plants before they are harvested.

When rice is almost ready to be harvested, it looks like this. Each tiny seed on the stalk is a piece of rice.

Or she might plant them right into the regular field. Then they just stay where they're planted. Some farmers plant the seeds by hand. They sprinkle the seeds over the ground without any machines.

Other farmers use machines. The machines take a seed and put it in the ground. Then they do it again and again. Machines are helpful on really big farms. They can plant a lot of rice in a short time.

On some really, really big farms, farmers plant the rice using an airplane! A plane flies over the field and drops the seeds to the ground. That's a really fast way of planting seeds.

34 **Rice**

GROWING UP

Rice grows for a few months. At first it looks like tiny blades of grass. The plant gets bigger and starts to look like giant grass.

While it's growing, the rice plant is green. After about three months it forms the rice. The rice is the seed of the plant. That's the part we eat. The rice looks like long lines of little bumps on **stalks**. Each bump is one rice seed.

The farmer drains the water out of the field when she sees the rice. The land has to be dry. The rice is almost ready to harvest.

HARVESTING

The rice is ready to harvest when the plants get brown. They won't be growing anymore after that.

On smaller farms, farmers harvest the rice by hand. They cut the stalks of the plant with knives. Then they lay the stalks out to dry.

On bigger farms, farmers use machines again. Machines cut down the plants. They split the rice from the stalks and leaves.

The rice is almost ready to travel on to people's tables. But there are a few more steps before it gets there. The journey from the farm to your plate is almost done!

CHAPTER FIVE

How Does Rice Get to Your Plate?

You might think that after rice is picked, it's all ready to be eaten. That's not quite true. There are still some more steps the rice has to go through before it's ready to eat.

THRESHING

Threshing is how people split the rice from the rest of the plant. Remember, after the farmer harvests it, the rice is still attached to the rest of the plant. There are extra leaves and stalks that we can't eat.

Farmers without machines thresh rice by hand. They might throw it around a little and catch the rice on a sheet on the ground. They might walk all over it. Or they might pound it with a special tool called a **mortar and pestle**.

Threshing by hand splits the rice from the rest of the plant. But it's still all mixed up on the ground or in a bowl.

This is a mortar and pestle. The mortar is a bowl usually made of wood or stone. The pestle is a heavy tool used to crush whatever is in the mortar.

38 Rice

These farmers are using a threshing machine to split the rice seeds from the rest of the plant. They put the rice plants into the thresher and wait for the seeds to come out.

The farmer usually throws the rice into the air. It's best if it's a windy day. The rice weighs a lot more than the other parts of the plant. The leaves and other parts blow away in the wind. The rice falls back into the bowl or onto the ground. After awhile, all that's left is the rice.

Farmers with machines don't thresh rice by hand. It takes a long time. If there is a lot of rice, the farmer would still be threshing by the time he had to plant the next round of seeds! Machines can split the rice from the leaves quickly.

DRYING

Right after the farmer harvests it, the rice has a lot of water in it. If it was sent to you right away, it would probably grow **mold**. Moldy rice isn't good to eat!

The farmer has to dry the rice first. He might just set it out in the sun. The rice is put onto pans and put in the field. Sometimes, a farmer can use a big drying machine to do it faster.

On larger farms, rice harvesting is done with these large machines. Once the rice is harvested it has to be threshed before going to the next steps on its trip to your plate.

40   Rice

THE HULL

Now the rice looks like a tiny seed with a wrapper on it. The wrapper is papery and brown. It's called the hull. People don't eat the hull. We can only eat the seed inside.

There are two ways to get the hull off the seed. You can take off the hull by hand. You can grind the rice between stones, or roll something over it. That loosens up the hull and it comes off.

This is when a lot of rice moves on to a factory. The factory gets the rice ready to be sent out to people who want to buy it. Lots of rice is hulled in a factory. Shelling machines take off the hulls.

At this point, the rice is brown rice. It's just the seed without the hull. Nothing else has to be done to it if it's going to stay brown rice.

MILLING AND ENRICHING

Milling is what makes brown rice into white rice. The brown rice goes through more machines and comes out as white rice.

One grain of rice has three parts. It has the **bran**, the **germ**, and the endosperm. Milling takes out the bran and the germ. All that's left is the endosperm. The endosperm is the white part of the rice inside. When you eat white rice, you're eating the endosperm part of the rice.

To become white rice, the three parts of rice have to be split apart. First, the brown rice goes through machines that take out the outer parts. Then it's cleaned up so it looks nice.

The bran and the germ have a lot of vitamins and minerals. White rice doesn't have those parts, so it doesn't have the vitamins and minerals either. Vitamins and minerals help to keep your body healthy.

Factories will put those vitamins and minerals back into white rice, though. Rice is often put into big tubs of vitamins and minerals. The rice soaks them up. Then they have to be dried again.

Finally, rice is put into packages. Some is put into big bags made out of a kind of plant. Some of it is put into smaller plastic bags.

GOING ON

Not much else has to happen to rice at the factory. If it's going to be made into a processed food, it will stay at the factory. Rice can be made into frozen dinners, or boxed meals. But most rice is just sold as rice.

There are many different kinds of rice. Some are long, some short. There are also different colors of rice, from white to brown to red.

 **42** **Rice**

A truck picks up the rice from the factory. It might bring it to a plane, boat, or train. Rice can travel a long way to get to customers!

Rice grown in China might end up in Europe. Rice grown in Latin America could end up in Canada. It has to cross oceans on planes and boats.

If the rice isn't going around the world, it might be sold nearby, or at least in the same country. The truck will take the rice from the factory and bring it to a grocery store warehouse.

A single warehouse stores and sorts food for a lot of different grocery stores. Workers unload the rice and split it up. The whole truckload of rice probably won't go to just one place. It will be split and sent to several stores.

AT THE STORE

From the warehouse, the rice gets sent to grocery stores. It's taken from another truck. Then workers put the rice on the shelves.

You and other customers walk by. You pick up your rice. But you probably have no idea where it came from!

Or at least, you didn't know before. Now, you know the story of your rice. You can even look on the bag to see exactly where it came from. It might be from China. Or India. Or Japan. Or Latin America. Check the label to see if you can find where your rice was grown!

DIFFERENT KINDS OF RICE

If you go to a grocery store with a lot of choices, you'll see just how many different kinds of rice there are!

First, there's white and brown rice. A lot of people like white rice because it cooks faster and stays good longer. Other people like brown rice because it has more vitamins and minerals in it. White rice has a lot less, so it's not as healthy for you.

Some rice is long and some is short. Long-grain rice is bigger and fluffy when you cook it. Short-grained rice is smaller and round, and sticks together when you cook it. Medium-grained rice is in between.

There is also wild rice. Wild rice grows in North America. It is not actually related to white or brown rice. Wild rice is a grain, but it's not the same grain. It does grow in water, though, just like most other rice.

The next time you're at the grocery store, think about all that food. Can you figure out its story? Look at the packages. Sometimes they give clues about where your food was grown.

You can also grow your own food. Or read more about it. If you ask more questions, you'll find out much more about just where your food comes from!

NOT JUST FOR FOOD

The rice plant is used for lots of things besides just eating the rice seed. After the rice is harvested, there's still a whole plant left. Farmers can feed it to animals. In Eastern Asia, people make the plant into hats and shoes. The husks and the rice itself can be put in mattresses. Laundry starch also comes from rice plants. So can paper, animal bedding, and more!

 **44** **Rice**

WORDS TO KNOW

bran: A piece of the outside of a seed that is pulled off before the seed is made into flour or other foods.

germ: A part of the outside of a seed pulled off with the bran during processing.

harvest: Gather grown plants on a farm.

ingredients: Foods that are mixed with others to make new foods.

irrigated: Watered fields using pipes.

mold: A fungus that grows on food.

mortar and pestle: A tool used for crushing up seeds or other plants. A mortar is a bowl. A pestle is shaped like a small club. Plants are kept in the mortar while someone can use the pestle to crush whatever is held in the bowl.

nutrients: Chemicals that living things need to eat in food to stay healthy.

products: Things people make, buy, and sell.

seedlings: Very small plants just starting to grow out of the ground.

soil: Dirt.

stalks: The main stems of a plant.

FIND OUT MORE

ONLINE

History for Kids: Rice
www.historyforkids.org/learn/food/rice.htm

International Year of Rice
www.fao.org/rice2004/en/kids.htm

Where Your Food Comes From
urbanext.illinois.edu/food

IN BOOKS

Reynolds, Jan. *Cycle of Rice, Cycle of Life*. New York: Lee and Low Books, 2009.

Sobol, Richard. *The Life of Rice: From Seedling to Supper*. Somerville, Mass.: Candlewick Press, 2010.

Veitch, Catherine. *Farms Around the World*. Mankato, Minn.: Heinemann-Raintree, 2011.

INDEX

ABOUT THE AUTHOR

Jane E. Singer is a freelance writer with several titles to her name. Singer writes about health, history, and other topics that affect young people. She is passionate about learning in and out of the classroom.

PICTURE CREDITS

Dreamstime.com:

    Anagr: p. 42

    Benigs: p. 40

    Blackphoenix1980: p. 14

    Bradcalkins: p. 31

    Carroteater: p. 34

    Cascoly: p. 30

    Chatchaiyo: p. 36

    Curaga: p. 6

    Digitalpress: p. 20

    Jeabjeab: p. 12

    Jojojojo: p. 32

    Juliengrondin: p. 26

    Kcphotos: p. 10

    Konstantin32: p. 29

    Leesniderphotoimages: p. 39

    Mangostock: p. 9

    Somchaip: p. 16

    Spaceport9: p. 23

    Stevemcsweeny: p. 22

    Thawats: p. 38

    Tomoki1970: p. 24

    Varandah: p. 18

    Vwvwvwvwv: p. 34